SAVE OUR LAND

by

Mary Ann Kalin

RoseDog Books
PITTSBURGH, PENNSYLVANIA 15238

RoseDog Books
585 Alpha Drive, Suite 103
Pittsburgh, PA 15238
Visit our website at *www.rosedogbookstore.com*

ISBN: 979-8-89211-307-6
eISBN: 979-8-89211-805-7

Take Care Of Our Land

There once was a large tree that stood straight and tall near the edge of a farm field where wheat, oats, or corn were planted on the land at different times passing year after year.

The tree branches held many leaves in the spring and summer months, that freshened the air.

The beautiful tree was cut down so houses could be built on that land. I wonder why the tree was not left there to stand and have the houses built around that tree for shade. We look at even one tree that provided shade and wonder why it had to be cut down.

Do we not take notice of things around us that were there before we were? Have we come to not keeping the farmers lands and crops, which have provided food and even milk that cows provided.

We are a great state and providers, however we are not taking care of our land. Some thought should be given to what we are doing.

This should not be all about us, one must consider what is taking place in the land.

THE TREE

THE LARGE OAK TREE WAS CUT DOWN, IT ONCE STOOD ON THE EDGE OF THE LAND NOW HOUSES STAND ON THE LAND

PLANET EARTH

PLANT EARTH HAS BEEN AROUND FOR
MANY WORLD GENERATIONS

THE ROADS

ROADS JOURNEY UP AND DOWN, FAST AND SLOW, TAKING US ON ROADS WE LIKE TO GO.

SUNSHINE

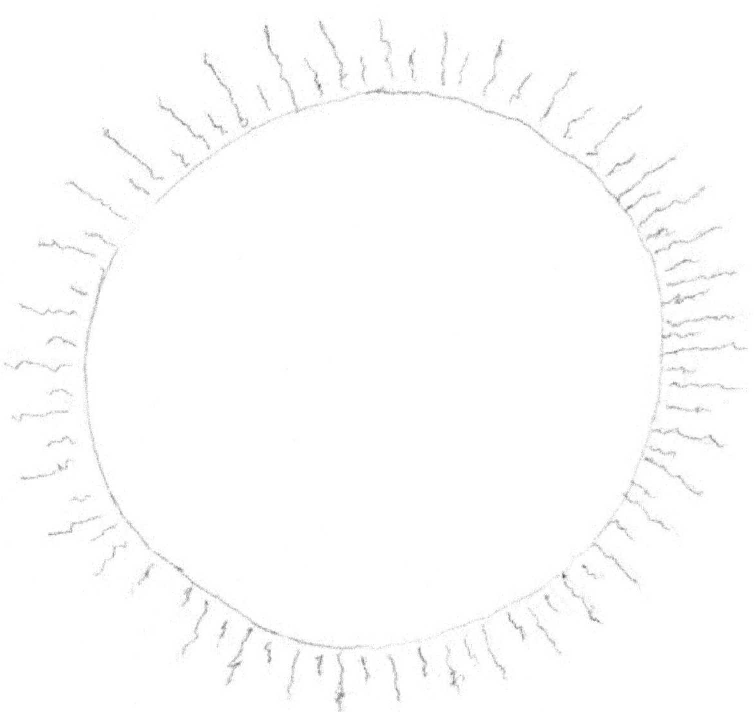

CLOUDS FLOAT HIGH IN THE SKY THE SUN SHINES BRIGHT
AND WARMS THE DAY.

THE MOON

THE MOON HOVERS OVER THE EARTH
GIVING LIGHT AT NIGHT

RAIN

RAIN DROPS GENTLY ON THE GROUND MAKING PUDDLES
WITHOUT A SOUND

CLOUDS

CLOUDS DRIFT GENTLY BY HIGH IN THE SKY

THE END